The
Bird
That
Swallowed
the
Music
Box

The Bird That Swallowed the Music Box

(Ways of Listening)

essays by

Anita Sullivan

Shanti Arts Publishing

Brunswick, Maine

The Bird That Swallowed the Music Box
(Ways of Listening)

Copyright © 2018 Anita Sullivan

Published by Shanti Arts Publishing

Cover and interior design by Shanti Arts Designs

Shanti Arts LLC
Brunswick, Maine
www.shantiarts.com

Printed in the United States of America

Cover illustration by Cary Loving
www.caryloving.com

"I Believe in the Existence of Strawberries," by Shimmy Boyle, appeared in *Blood Orange Review* in April 2013 and is here used with the permission of the poet.

ISBN: 978-1-947067-46-2 (softcover)
ISBN: 978-1-947067-47-9 (digital)

LCCN: 2018948884

For Ted

Acknowledgments

"Scordatura: Upon Listening to Biber's *Rosary Sonatas*" was published in *Image*, Summer 2009, Issue 62; and also in *The Best Spiritual Writing 2011*, Philip Zaleski (editor), Penguin Books, 2010.

"The Physicality of Language" was published in *VoiceCatcher*, 2013.

"The Song of Songs" was included as an Afterword in *The Song of Songs: Codes of Love*, Edwin M. Good, Cascade Books, 2015.

All other essays were originally published in *The Weekly Hubris.* <www.weeklyhubris.com>

Contents

On the Bus:
Anecdote into Story

During the past year, I've been riding the city bus quite often to keep from using the car. This puts me in touch with what you might call a representative swatch of the community. Mostly, I ride back and forth to the library and the nearby city-center grocery store, which has the best deli in town.

This is the core of the city, where people of all ages sit smoking and leaning against their backpacks, some holding up cardboard signs, others busking with guitars or ukuleles, or just plain hanging out. Speakers have been placed high on the outside walls of the library directly across from the bus station, prepared to broadcast classical music (mostly opera) in case the lingering groups of street people become too numerous or unruly.

It's a pretty typical urban center of a contemporary middle-sized metropolis.

Many of the people I see on the bus are obviously not doing very well: they hobble, waddle, jerk spasmodically, or mutter to themselves. Yet rarely do I see anyone forget to offer a courteous "thank you" to the bus driver or show a general polite awareness to their fellow passengers. Each bus is a small clot of living mythologies, tracing its infrared pattern daily around the city.

Because I'm a writer, I ache to know the stories of every person on the bus, my weird and wonderful fellow humans, each one dragging her little shop of horrors behind her like an invisible burlap sack.

But what I want to know is not what they would be able to tell me.

"Anecdote" means "unpublished," (from the Greek *an-ekdota*) which means informal, without shape or polish. Your own story is and must be exactly that: a work in progress, connected to you like a Siamese twin, and thus never "done" enough to let loose, even if you've told parts of it many times before. An anecdote is so private that it's doomed to fail at the things that a story can best be: free and artful.

So, if some stranger manages to sit you down and tell you "a story," which almost certainly means a segment of his or her ongoing life, the result can be disappointing, and you're not always sure exactly why, even if it's filled with the same kind of drama, pain, pathos, triumphs, and failures you would see in print or on the screen.

On the bus, what I really want is the "published" — the *ekdota* — version of each of these people's lives. But paradoxically, that means I want the real story. You'd think no matter how much else a person is lacking, at least that's the one thing only they know best. But no, we really only know the anecdotal version of our lives. The nonfiction version, if you will, is "true" as far as it goes, but doomed in the telling to be forever incomplete. There is absolutely no way that a person can truly, completely tell his story. Somebody else has to do it.

An anecdote is like a candidate for sainthood. After being properly vetted, verified, probed, polished, and ornamented with festoons of other possibilities that could have happened instead, the anecdote may finally break loose from its teller and become a full "story candidate." Now it can roam the streets with its credentials, hoping to attract the "story river monster" who comes along to gobble up such recruits. Only then can it enter the crucible and eventually emerge fully formed.

A finished story tells itself. It is a whole world. If somebody starts to spin you a yarn on the bus or in the living room or around the kitchen table in a conversation, even if it has a really bizarre plot, the problem is that the teller already knows the ending. And you, the listener, know that she knows. Therefore, there's no secret. End of story.

So, as I ride the bus, I'm in turmoil. I long to

know, very specifically, who these people are and what it would take to make their stories have a happy ending. I long to pluck each festering anecdote from its owner and hand it over to the story monster. Instead, all I can do is listen, watch, be courteous, and go home to the people I know with renewed humility and love . . . and try to write down as much as I've learned before I forget.

Turtles and Candles: A New Folklore in the Making?

If you come across a turtle in the middle of the road when you're out walking or driving, what do you do? Probably go around it, right?

No need to be afraid, unless you elect to pick it up with your bare hands to keep it from getting run over, and it turns out to be a snapping turtle. On a hiking trail, you might stop to peer at the pattern on its back and smile at its pudgy little feet and strange head, but then you'd go on your way.

Most turtles we see are small enough that they would certainly not remind us of the original tortoise who was given the task of carrying the entire Earth on its back. This worked out because the world was mostly water then, and the only way the earth could stay dry enough was if somebody held it up. The tortoise, being totally comfortable in water—forget the distinction between "turtle" and "tortoise," which in folklore is truly irrelevant—and with such a durable back, was perfect for the job.

Aside from holding up the world, though, turtles don't show up in stories nearly as often as lions, bears, or rabbits. Even among reptiles, the turtle takes second place to the frog, snake, dragon, dinosaur, or lizard; it simply doesn't have the mythological heft of its cousins, real or imagined.

So, I wonder how many of us, gazing down at a real turtle by our feet, would immediately think: "Such a lovely, flat surface. What a perfect spot for a candle!"

Yet I recently came across three separate literary references to a turtle walking around with a burning candle on its back. Naturally, I assumed it must be an old folk tale, and I looked it up online.

But Wikipedia is silent on the topic, if "topic" is the right word. The three writers in whose work I found this exact same image all claim to have made it up. Two of the three stories came from Greece, yet there seems to be no folk tradition behind it. All I can say is "HUH?"

After all, if this can happen with turtles, what else might it happen with?

It could be a hopeful sign of something.

Here I present my three, totally disparate examples of the turtle-candle story.

First, the long one:

In a 1994 Greek novel, They Come Back in Wolf Light, by Ziranna Zatelli (never published in English translation), the title of one chapter is "The winds were blowing from the four corners, and a turtle was going along with a candle on its back." A beloved and delightful little girl has just died somewhat mysteriously, likely of polio, but there is a suggestion that she was spirited away. The chapter opens with the mourning ritual, during which the extended family sits up all night exchanging their memories of the child. The grief-stricken mother is talking obsessively, almost non-stop, and the other family members finally appeal to her father-in-law, the family patriarch, to calm her down. "Tell the story about the tortoise with the candle on its back," his wife suggests. So he does.

In the story, a child has also died, and a lady turtle prepares to go to the funeral to pay her respects. She is polite and wishes to bring a suitable offering. Most mourners arrive carrying candles, so she heads down the road with a lighted candle on her back— never mind how it got there. Along the way, everybody who sees Mrs. Turtle absolutely cracks up in laughter at how ridiculous she looks. But the timid, polite little animal keeps plodding along. Finally, she reaches the room of the dead child, where the mother is weeping over the body. People are horrified because they're afraid if the mother sees the turtle, she might cheer up. And sure enough, when the mother turns to look, she begins to laugh.

The moral of the story is that it's a good thing to encourage laughter at funerals.

Second, a shorter example:

In a recent mystery novel by Peter Helton, An Inch of Time, a group of foreign artists have moved into a deserted village on the Greek island of Corfu. Strange accidents keep happening to them, as if the residents of the next village are trying to scare them away. In one incident, they wake up in the middle of the night smelling smoke and discover a set of small fires in the dry grass around their rambling old villa. As they go out to investigate, they discover a random group of tortoises wandering around the grounds, all with lighted candles on their backs, unwittingly setting fire to the place.

When I wrote to Helton to ask him if he knew about Zatelli's novel or if he had heard this little fable somewhere in Greece, he wrote back and said no, he had totally made it up. "It just seemed like a really good way to set fire to a Greek village," said this novelist. Mystery writers, after all, do have their standards!

Third, a poem showed up about two years ago in the online poetry journal *Blood Orange Review*. I liked the poem because I'm a fan of the contemporary style that's loosely called "surrealism," but I couldn't help but notice the turtle-candle part. When I wrote to the author asking if he had gotten this image from Greek folklore or, indeed, anywhere else, he said no, he had made it up. Somewhat more understandable that a random image would occur to a poet, of course, but I am still actively puzzled.

Here, by the way, is the poem, whose author is Shimmy Boyle, a San Francisco Bay area performance poet:

I Believe in the Existence of Strawberries

There are turtles sleeping in a garden somewhere
While candles burn on top of their shells
And an old record plays the blues
And two people dance
As though one of their bodies is the sky
And the other
The Storm sweeping across it

Like many people interested in folklore and myth—especially the quirky mini-stories hidden as details within the larger plots, details we take as bedrock truth, and hold onto as strongly and sincerely as if they were religious beliefs or established customs—I always wonder: "Where did this come from?" And now, maybe we are looking at a folk truth in its infancy, one that could grow stronger and begin to emerge as a totally new plot variation, or, more likely, will be absorbed as a version of a much larger story already in place. Keep your eyes and ears open!

The Bird That Swallowed the Music Box

Tell me, when in total silence the local forest thrushes begin to assemble and to look about themselves on early summer evenings, does this small preliminary ritual, repeated so often during their singing season, does it *shape* the song that then occurs around the folded feathers of them?

Each bird in its territory sings by note into phrase, by phrase into measure, and by measure into the fullness of an improvised fractal composition. How do they stay sane enough to continue without knowing they are unique among birds and are precisely splitting each new outburst of melody as if it were a seed? This on each evening for the month or two during which they are moved to sing.

I am a merry-go-round manikin yanked by the pole at the top of my head and tossed off the wheel. My pole goes into the soft ground. I see the whirling stars beneath my chin. I hear that foolish bird, the ancient one, swallow the music box when a lesser god tossed it out of an airplane like a pop bottle into the jungle. It never hit the ground. The First Thrush opened its beak — a whir and click — and the process was begun.

A little breeze passes through the pine woods and the Swainson's thrush flies to a closer branch. My vertical ear slowly fills again, like an oil lamp; the song, beautiful.

Deep in the brown bird's throat is a music box. Yes, but it has long stopped, has flattened into silver sheets as thin as parchment through which might be seen the shape of the machine that strangled the original bird from the inside out. Each evening, not theme and variation, only theme. Beginning again. Listen!

The ancient bird's voice darkened with blood and pain. For centuries it could not stop spewing clots as the music box slowly unwound, clearing its windpipe, another hollow bone.

Do they now — the entire thrush tribe on summer evenings centuries later — still split voice as if it were a seed so a song may be permitted, at the very least, to reappear as its music box version would have done? How can I, a human, remember this chained song in its entirety when it has not yet cooled, thickened, and slipped tear-shaped from the pipette throat, unless I assume it is beautiful for the wrong reason, as I have always done?

The Physicality of Language: From Hand to Mouth

I – Chaucer Stirs Things Up

One evening I sat in the audience at a poetry reading, waiting for it to start. Other people were talking quietly, but I wasn't conversing or paying attention to individual words, only aware of the general hum. Then from directly behind me, a voice began to speak slowly in a hoarse whisper:

> Whan that Aprill with his shoures soote
> The droghte of March hath perced to the roote,
> And bathed every veyne in swich licour . . .

The first three lines from the "Prologue" of

Chaucer's *Canterbury Tales* were being spoken in beautiful Middle English dialect.

Immediately my body began to shake beyond my control, and my eyes filled with tears. I could hardly breathe. This was a very different reaction from the one I would soon be having when I listened to two poets read their contemporary lines.

I didn't turn around to see who was behind me. The uncanny whisper ended abruptly after these three lines and never resumed for the rest of the evening. But I was stunned by the simple, almost brutal physicality of my response, as if I actually had been touched by these words. After I got home, I felt a need to think about the experience.

In what way can words alone become so physical? Daily we exercise our human capacity to emit, absorb, and shape a variety of sounds with our ears, mouths, chests, stomachs. We are physically involved in regularly altering air. Words themselves are not objects. Yet listening to three lines of Chaucer at that particular moment was for me the same as being struck in the solar plexus by a stone. It was like my entire body being rubbed, inside and out, with something uniquely rough and prickly. I had a physical reaction to those words that did not come from their meaning, nor from some passing resemblance to noises of predators, weapons, or the mesmerizing rhythms of drum beats.

Several persistent questions refused to go away: Was this just a fluke brought about by an odd combination of circumstances? Did this happen in the past quite often? If so, where, when, why? Why doesn't it happen any more?

Mine was not a secondary reaction first processed by the conscious mind; it had little or nothing to do with meaning, rhythm, meter, assonance, alliteration, rhyme. This felt much farther down the brain stem ladder toward the visceral . . . and yet more refined at the same time.

I had been unaccountably catapulted into some kind of earlier human relationship with language, and it was neither a simple nor an unmindful one.

Chaucer's words had to do with spring. Therefore, my response may have been preconditioned to be stronger than if he had been talking about a divorce or a fishing trip. Nevertheless, some combination of meaning, sound, rhythm, and the particular situation conjured for me an original emotional experience and was not simply evoked as the memory of a previous one.

Speaking as a poet, I have come to recognize that raw emotions are like rare natural resources: They must be actively mined through some extraction process with tools. They do not obey ordinary verbal commands or cues any more than volcanoes and hurricanes do, and like weather gods, their powers should not be fooled with. Not surprisingly, humans seem to be constructed much like Earth itself: We have a seething central core, well insulated from the surface by various levels of relatively opaque matter — our brains, for example! But there are vents through which the steam is regularly allowed to release. I believe the ritual of oral storytelling and poetry was one of those vents and one of poetry's original functions. It is a function now basically obsolete.

And yes, my brief experience with the first few words in Chaucer's amazing poem was related to spring, and through the propelling "juice" of this season, I came into the rhetorical space that ancient poetry used to carve out for itself whenever people gathered for important rites and ceremonies. I could feel a seething in his words; I could feel the ancient, collective urgency and "riddlic fire" moving through his lines. I was connecting with the enormous tradition in ancient myth and story in which words, under the right conditions, can have actual power to bring new matter into the world, rather than simply serving as a stamp of identification and approval afterward.

So the first thing I settled in my mind was that my physical reaction was not because I was remembering some event in my own past, one that the words had brutally yanked from my poor quivering unconscious mind. Poetry can do that too. But this was not about me. This was much older, like the language of original naming.

II - From Syllables to Names

If we're going to treat words as if they are physical objects instead of mere puffs of air, we need to go way back in time to when people actually believed this sort of thing. In the ancient Hindu mythology of India, for example, the huge crossover from Nothing into Something was brought about by an "object" that resembled the sub-atomic particles of modern physics; that is, it was so "small" that people couldn't perceive it with their senses but only with their imaginations. And that object, too small to see with any magnifying device, too teensy to finger-roll like a grain of sand, they called the "syllable."

In the typical paradoxical fashion of Vedic myth, the syllable — the very first physical object in the universe — was refined into existence by listing everything it is not:

> It is neither thick nor thin, neither short nor long, neither flame nor liquid, neither colored nor dark, neither wind nor ether; it doesn't stick, is without taste, without smell, without eyes, without ears, without voice, without mind, without heat, without breath, without mouth, without measure, without an inside, without an outside. It does not eat and is not eaten. (Roberto Calasso, *Literature and the Gods*, 2001)

Here, mythology and science are in agreement: this "object" is impossible to imagine, much less talk about, without resorting to metaphor. You have to make a second thing before you find out what is actually there first. It's like kids with mud pies. Fueled by the energy of mindless enthusiasm, they start digging into the muck and scooping stuff out. Then they pile that stuff somewhere else, and the place they started with turns into a hole. The hole is different from the new pile they have made. There's no way to make something new without having two things going on at the same time.

Then what happens, of course, is that we all lose track of what is "first" because it never really was the issue. So we're left forever with both metaphor and whatever else we have also discovered . . . or made. This is the gods' dilemma as well as ours.

Flash forward to our own era when we have achieved a full separation between the physical and the spiritual, between the hard and the soft, the real and the imagined. Our syllables have glommed themselves into words, and these, though they have motivating power, we place firmly on the non-physical side of the spreadsheet. For us, words possess only the relatively soft and temporary power that comes through meaning, or at best, through the sounds and rhythms we might hear from preachers, politicians, poets, and the like. While words might incite physical action, they do not possess the heft of the original syllable, which in the Vedic myth was also the footprint of an enormous cow.

Yet words are not totally non-material, are they? Spoken and written, they involve breath, shape, volume, and the weight of our hands.

As early humans huffed and spewed syllables and other vocal noises into speech, something like a word-attention capacity must have grown inside us until it swelled into a small appendage. Maybe we came to count on our words so much that we forgot that the rest of the world also has a language.

At the very least, the new requirements of listening in a different way to one another — shall we say, talking more and more about less and less — would have privileged the latent and subversive power of passive voice, going back to the time when we stood in the Garden of Eden being named. This is the part that has fallen out of our origin myth: that initial moment when "we" felt the weight of our own animal name come gently down upon us like a cloak of office. I like to think that this act occurred with all our senses simultaneously combined into an enormous symphony of receiving, a kind of full-species epiphany.

Soon enough we stepped out from the flat background of our former existence into a resonant space. We became anointed ones, beings who could simultaneously listen to and speak . . . words.

So stunning was this awakening of human consciousness that it hovers as a persistent theme in various mythologies, especially as a tale in which a creator god builds a set of living beings (like mud pies!), only to recognize, belatedly, that these creatures know as much as he does. Reluctant to destroy his beautiful creatures, he has to figure out a way to dumb us down. In many Central American native mythologies, this is done by clouding the eyes of humans so they can no longer see as far as the gods, metaphorically expressed as "breath on the mirror."

Eventually, we newly anointed word-wielders began to name everything that was not us.

But naming was not as simple as it sounds. We didn't just line up all physical objects into a row like soldiers and bark out a single noun for each. We all know there is more to language than just nouns. Words can shapeshift back and forth from verbs to nouns to adjectives, and everybody who has ever tried to learn a foreign language knows that people speak in phrases, in "clumps" of sounds, not in individual words.

And finally, here comes metaphor again. In early times, people apparently did not separate their language from their mythology. If a man in Siberia mentioned a branch near a fire, he might use a word we'd translate as "gnarled stick." But the term he was using referred simultaneously to the kettle hanging from the branch and the whole surrounding area; its full meaning would be "the hearth of the horned mother-universe."

A Tzutujil Maya talking about a thirsty jaguar would refer to the animal as "a woman's child of the Old Complete Being searching for the mouth of Our Mother because of the sharpness of Our Father's Teeth." Names were not abstract; they were connected to an entire worldview with its long trail of stories.

This "packed" quality of words is beautifully expressed by the poet Osip Mandelstam:

> Any given word is a bundle, and meaning sticks out of it in various directions, not aspiring toward any single official point. In pronouncing the word "sun," we are, as it were, undertaking an enormous journey to which we are so accustomed that we travel in our sleep. What distinguishes poetry from automatic speech is that it rouses us and shakes us into wakefulness in the middle of a word. Then it turns out that the word is much longer than we thought, and we remember that to speak means to be forever on the road. ("Conversation About Dante," 1933)

Our language began as a bundle. Every named object contained, curled inside, the enormous nuclear-fission power of its story. In their way of speaking, people in early societies acknowledged that certain fragments of that story would remain concealed and potent, like a compressed spring hidden by cloth or stone.

I believe language continues to conceal much of itself in exactly the fierce, bristling way described above, but in order to release the catch on its sprung powers, we probably need to treat it more like a wild animal than a pet.

III - From Hand to Mouth

Sticks and stones may break my bones
But names will never hurt me

To regard language as physical, we need to notice our own weight in the world. We are more than the mere lumps we would be if "being" were the only verb and "doing" did not exist. For humans, developing the capacity for language involved additional ways of doing, with both our voices and gestures.

A common assumption is that human language was oral long before it was written. Many mythologies privilege "the Word" as the origin of the universe, by which they usually mean a sound as well as a meaning (a different idea from the Sanskrit syllable). If we assume language is a thing that can have a beginning and we also assume humans existed for a while without it, then at some point a unique human attention capacity was mysteriously activated by something we were doing with our bodies, not just our voices. We began to feel the tension between the "soft power" of meaning and the spontaneous daily physical acts of bellowing, grunting, clapping, gesturing, jumping, grimacing, pointing, hissing, etc.

For some reason, we began to want more specific results from these familiar gestures and noises. Gradually we worked them into a full-bore language. Our voices especially seemed to intrigue us, so we taught ourselves to sing and to pronounce. At the same time, though, we were dreaming up new tasks for our hands.

So far as we know, humans have been making meaningful marks with their fingers dipped into various gooey mixtures for countless eons. We've also used tools to scratch marks onto sticks, bones, and rocks. We have drawn lines in the dirt but also onto just about any surface that would sustain the impression, including, of course, our own bodies.

People all over the world who do what we call "rock art" — in Australia going back at least 50,000 years and possibly of a similar age in parts of Africa — have generally called it "writing" rather than "art." There is no consensus among archaeologists, art historians, and the participants themselves as to what these marks signify, but it is generally assumed that they were not random doodling exercises.

Rather, people were communicating something either local and practical — "Here is a dangerous whirlpool"; "There's water in a little tunnel nearby"; "This is where the landslide happened seventeen moons ago" — or were speaking a kind of pidgin-code that allowed adjacent groups to exchange information without speaking the same language. They may also have been communicating with the spirit world.

All of this was language, but it was silent — analogous to sign language perhaps — but in any case a visual code to make complex connections with other people, with the larger world, and with the cosmos. I believe that writing and speaking developed simultaneously, neither "emerging" from the other, but superimposed, intertwined in a huge variety of ways. This allows for a kind of whole-body understanding of our language development rather than confining it mostly to our heads.

Besides rock writing and other meaningful marks on objects hard and soft, there exists an entire language of gesture that we inherit and practice from our pre-hominid ancestors; we loosely refer to it as "body language." Gesture is refined into a highly articulate speech called sign language, and who is to say that humans with full hearing capacity did not communicate this way, deliberately and with great complexity, in many early cultures? Dance, mime, the martial arts, and entire sets of specialized, coded motion patterns (tea ceremonies, for example) offer ways for humans to extend the physicality of language beyond the vocal.

The silent part of our speaking, though, especially involves the hands with their huge complex of nerve-endings, tendons, and skin sensitivities. Axel Munthe, a Swedish physician who wrote a bestseller in 1929 about his life, *The Story of San Michele*, was awed by the mute healing power of the human hand. Speaking of his dying patients, he said:

> *Why, even after the power of speech had gone and the terror of death was staring out of their eyes, did they become so peaceful*

and still when I laid my hand on their forehead?

And then, this wise physician continued:

> One day, one of my best friends [then in the lunatic asylum] hit me on the back of the head with a hammer he had got hold of in some inexplicable way, and I was carried unconscious to the infirmary. It was a terrible blow, my friend was an ex-blacksmith who knew his business. . . . As I lay there in the infirmary a whole week with an icebag on my "head of a bear" and no visitors or books to keep me company, I began to think hard on the subject, and not even the blacksmith's hammer could make me abandon my theory that it was all in the hand.

At this point I feel myself wanting to shout "from hand to mouth!" and here's why: The human hand is amazingly sensitive in both giving and receiving the highest and most concentrated of human energies. Dumbly it moves across surfaces, and explosions take place inside our bodies.

"Things have their secrets," said Heraclitus over two thousand years ago. "What you touch knows what you think," wrote poet Daniela Elza in 2013, as if in reply. And more recently, continuing this conversation, Finnish architect Juhani Pallasmaa, author of a book called *The Thinking Hand*, said in an interview, "There is a rather wide agreement in science that our amazing hands are not products of our spectacular brains, but we have our amazing brains due to our spectacular hands."

Through eons of "handiwork," through a variety of finely practiced acts of touching, the hand — the healer's, the laborer's, the lover's, the artist's — has acted as a transformer, taking in the unvoiced secrets of things and transferring the shape, form, force, and full body of them into an emotional response within us. We are then able, with our minds, to translate that response into words. Voila! We have changed one element into another; we have made electricity from coal and fire; we have translated the physical world into language.

IV - Chaucer Has the Last Word

For this was on Seynt
Valentynes day
When every foul cometh ther
to chese his make,
Of every kind, that men thenke may

So Chaucer says, midway through his poem "Parliament of Fowls" as he launches into a kind of naming frenzy or catalogue of all the birds who have come together to choose their "makes" (mates). The last line has been translated as "all kinds that have a name that men can say," and also "of every species that men know, I say." In any case, and looking back to the original above, it seems to me the words contain a tantalizing ambivalence, an implication that naming is a limited power, which could imply that there is more to language than just an endless telling.

Here, in the final section, I want to return to the original conclusions I allowed myself to jump to after reacting so strongly to a few lines from the opening of Chaucer's *Canterbury Tales*: 1) Words sometimes seem to bypass the mind and affect a person as if they had been touched, shaken, punched, lightly stroked, etc.; 2) That language can, will, and should routinely have such a direct, hands-on power is knowledge that humans once shared but lost somewhere in either history or prehistory.

Let me address these issues again with a final question: When do words become a new experience instead of simply evoking, narrating, or describing a previous one?

For such an experience to happen, I believe the timing needs to be exactly right. A crack needs to open between what is spoken and what is understood. This, of course, happens almost every time people talk to each other, but mostly we shrug it off because we assume language will smooth over the cracks. Now and then, though, we need to notice that crack just at the moment it's closing and to be puzzled enough to keep it open just a fraction of a second longer than usual.

During that brief time, two possible outcomes tremble in the balance: We relax and figure, oh well, once again we've mis-understood — I thought you said "a searing man," when, of course, you must have said "a seated man" — or we recognize that a new arrangement of events has just occurred — "Yes, my ex-husband did have a certain kind of vigor, come to think of it" — and seize a rare opportunity to expand our precious cache of experiential knowledge.

This can be painful, like getting a shot or even a blood transfusion.

If you think about it, how often do you actually learn something that doesn't involve simply connecting another link to what you already know? Once a person grows into adulthood, the "tacking-on" way of learning has become so ingrained that we easily fall in with it, not realizing that it carries, as a side effect, a kind of numbness.

Hearing the opening lines of Chaucer's "Prologue" allowed me to re-experience an initial connection with the world. I felt as if I were being offered a gift, neither despite nor because of how I had led my life. I heard these words as the first way that something essential would be spoken. The words filled the crack like a physical continuation of what they were speaking about, and I could fully take it in. It was like a beautiful embrace; no, it was a beautiful embrace.

Well, of course, there is no way to experience something for the first time more than once! To realize, even briefly, that an original physicality to words after so many centuries of developing a more distant relationship must involve the prefix "re-" (as in "remember," "renew," "redundant," "repeat"). But blessedly, since the "we" that each individual person embodies is historically prone to spells of communal forgetting, I believe humans have lived for centuries in a chronic state of depletion — spiritual, imaginal, visionary, all of the above — without realizing it. It's almost as if we grew up too fast or came out of the garden too soon.

So easily, if we allow ourselves, can we drop into a childlike "Garden of Eden" frame of mind. I believe each of us harbors such a "place" deep within ourselves. Yet this is not the same as a *tabula rasa* because each human does come into the world already possessed of an enormous "basic education," a set of structural and topographical intuitions we've imbibed and even honed while in the womb that continue to develop at a rather wild rate for at least the first few years of our lives. Because this part of us has never named anything, it holds the innocent power of perpetual readiness. In order to learn something truly new, it is probably necessary to find a way back to this place where a passionate curiosity consumes us utterly, yet we are not impatient; we're ready and willing to keep reconfiguring the world. This theme occurs in many stories and legends; for example, the Parsival tales of medieval Europe.

By luck or by accident, we can find our way

into that place of wildness inside ourselves and hear old words spoken as if for the first time. And although we are accustomed to consider "language" to refer only to spoken and written words, which in themselves pack a wallop less than a wet noodle, a person might yet seek out and feel the sparking that happens each time the crack closes between worlds. It is in this split-second range of almost-not, not-quite, just-before, could-have-been-something-else-just-as-easily, didn't I just fly for three seconds? . . . it is here where the marvelous hammer blow of essential enchantment lies.

Clocking Memory

And if there is a silence that falls inside certain
words, when, how, with what violence does
that take place, and what difference does it
make to who you are?
                    — Anne Carson (Nay Rather)

Lying in bed in a silent room I am hearing the
voice of my grandfather's clock as if it were striking
downstairs and the sound coming up.

This clock, a family heirloom that is both
a grandfather and once was my grandfather's,
occupies a corner in the living room of my house,
broken, unrepaired, and unplugged—a largish
piece of furniture deprived of its useful function.
And before we moved to this house, it endured a
previous eight-year stint of enforced silence in the
corner of a friend's dining room because I—its
designated caretaker—had no space for it in my
apartment. A sequence of long spells during which

I do not hear this clock at all stretches through the capillaries of memory, back to my childhood, when the clock spoke regularly and with dignified authority in the entry hall of my grandparents' house.

This is a family clock that I inherited by default (nobody else would take it) and that I love. But the total number of hours that its regular striking has been part of my daily life have been pitifully few.

And yet, on this one normal morning before the day begins, I have been suddenly and unaccountably wakened by the small, precise, fluid, metal voice of the clock, speaking to me from the parallel world of deep memory. There is no way I could deliberately call to mind this sweet noise so clearly. I am hearing, not imagining, the full round of its preordained set of tones, and the sensation is one of total familiarity more than anything else. Not surprise, not beauty, but "Oh, yes, you." This is actual, not narrative memory: its story occurs only in present time, the time of the living.

The sweet uniqueness of that voice curls slowly through the room and my inner ear shifts position to follow it, as if I were watching a butterfly floating past and turning only my head to keep it in view.

I do not actually hear anything; the sound was not triggered, more dislodged. Like a helium birthday balloon held firmly in place for days with a plastic clothespin fixed to its ribbon, then freed to continue its interrupted journey to the ceiling. My dear clock has unfinished business to attend to, and I seem to be in its path.

This at a time when the sodden stupidities of thousands of years of human civilization are converging into a climax so terrible that Earth may soon totter into its Sixth Extinction. Awareness of this possibility is a small coin of lead that for many of us has added an extra and unnatural weight on our hearts for so long now that we have completely forgotten those unpredictable visitations of totally unreasonable happiness that surely are a normal part of being fully human.

Yet on this ordinary morning, my clock and my bones fell into a rare collaboration, something that surely must not be wholly physical (are my eardrums actually throbbing?) but just as surely is wholly present: the enhanced cellular memory of the delicately calibrated sounds made by a complicated set of brass gears and pulleys behind a rectangular face. Surely this machine is speaking — has always spoken — some necessary thing I will understand more fully at a later time. But there may be no later time, and only half awake, I will go out not knowing.

I do not understand this memory, which has arrived solely by grace, but the sound of the clock inside my body has lifted the coin of lead for awhile, floated it up a few inches, where now it hovers. Like a desert seed that lies dormant for weeks, months, even years, but nonetheless will swell into growth at the simple touch of sufficient water, my heart briefly resumes an old habit of natural joy.

A Weedy Taxonomy

Every spring I am confronted with one of my most annoying weaknesses: I never can remember the names of common plants, especially the weeds. Birds are no problem. I can identify a bird half hidden in a bush by size, shape, the way it moves, and sometimes by its small private mutterings.

It took years of practice to develop these instincts, but I hardly noticed. I was having so much fun.

But now I earnestly want to do the same with the familiar plants that are sprouting and blooming all around my feet everywhere I go: the plants otherwise known as "weeds." I want to know which weeds are edible, just in case there is an earthquake and my neighbors and I are reduced to scrounging for food in the yards of the houses we used to live in before they became mere piles of useless rubble.

Besides, why don't we know the names of the hundreds of common plants that appear in meadows, in woods, and in yards all over town every spring, sending up delicate, minuscule flowers on the ends of long spindly stems, sending out thousands of tiny leaves that might give us essential vitamins if we had sense enough to pick them and put them into soups or salads? When did we stop considering this to be basic and essential information, so basic that it could be passed along through the "child grapevine," that is, from child to child without the intervention of parents?

So, on a warm sunny day in early March, I headed into the woods with some trepidation: what will my percentage be this year? All the notes I made last year in the margins of my plant guides, the careful drawings of leaves, will I have forgotten most of it during the winter, again? Instead of looking up into the trees and into the bushes as I did for so many years, searching for birds, now my focus is much closer and lower down. I peer at tiny leaves: how many lobes? Are they toothed, shiny, do they have hairs on the back, are they involute or not? What family does each plant belong to, and what does that family like to do on warm spring evenings?

It's like wading into a swamp. "Too late!" says the voice in my head. "You can't even tell dandelion from cat's ear from chicory in your own backyard." Aiee! the mints and the mustards and the mallows are myriad. Everywhere I look there is a familiar plant whose name I have been told many times, but I can't figure out a way to make the name stick in my head. Arghh!

Then as I was coming back down the path from the summit of the trail, I had a subversive thought. Maybe the problem is not the names themselves, the problem is that somebody else made up these names. I was looking at northern bedstraw as I had this thought. It's that spindly vine with skinny little leaves lined up evenly on both sides, and it sticks to you when you wander off the path into the woods. It's a very opportunistic weed, but really kind of pathetic, thinking it can hitch a ride on your jeans and start a new life somewhere else. That's its own signature survival tactic; every plant has one.

Can you imagine the thousands of plant board meetings that must have taken place since the Lower Cretaceous with heated discussions regarding optimum coping strategies? How to Attract Pollinators, How to Spread Seeds, Depth of Roots, Drought Resistance, Water Storage and Disbursal, How to Keep from Being Eaten, Beetle Management, etc., etc. The solutions are staggeringly cunning, effective and numerous.

But at that particular moment, looking at this weed, I could remember its personality, quirks, and habits, but I could not call up its name. So I decided to make one up. Why not? If you make up your own name for a weed you're actually familiar with, then you're likely to think of the weed and the name as a single unit. Later, if you can substitute the real name for the one you made up, you'll still have the whole unit. That's the secret to remembering plant names.

I had probably just re-invented one of the many mnemonic methods taught by Giordano Bruno and other genius heretics in the sixteenth century when people still memorized large chunks of text for a variety of reasons.

So, I called the northern bedstraw "the running footman." By the end of my hike I had named a couple of others too: "grandmother looks out three windows" is my name for snakeroot, and "drying long fingernails" turns out to be sheep sorrell. Naturally I must be cautious with my naming technique, or else I will be merely taxing my brain with an entire new layer of Forgotten Names. Making the transfer from the personal to the properly botanical should happen much more easily if I take the time to form a close and complicated relationship with each plant, so that its name is not just a label, but a part of its full identity. What I hope is that when I do actually, firmly, and securely identify each of these plants by its "real name," then every time I see the plant, the name I made up will quietly become like the "key" that allows me always to unlock that word.

Only about a thousand more weeds to go, and I'll be ready for the earthquake.

Honking

Unlike most birds who pour into the air complete vocal masterpieces honed by evolution, Raven has been chosen as the one to emit what in the final annals of the world will be listed as HONK. This important slot in the index has been held open for him for a long time.

Yes, Raven is meant to do the Honk, which he's always trying to perfect, which he's always trying out a brand new version of, but that never quite works. But we stop and listen every time he flies over because we can hear his lordly mind working up there, convinced that this latest set of tentative (dare I say feeble?) airborne croaks is the real thing, at last, at last.

And if it were, it would indeed be magnificent.
Does anything, then, actually Honk?
Well, no. Not yet.

Raven makes many different calls, but they all sound as if he's practicing for an ultimate one that will happen differently, later.

Sometimes the sound he makes seems to be muffled by leather, so that he is a bird *creaking* overhead. The world darkens imperceptibly, in disappointment.

Long ago, Raven and his call seem to have been separated, so each of them wanders orphaned in the world, looking for the other. Sometimes he flies over, emitting the kind of sound that usually happens inside the oarlock of a rowboat, as if he came out of the egg in a cave where he could produce enormous resonances with very little effort. The proportions were wrong. The space itself was doing most of the work, so when he emerged into the larger world, it was as if his throat had shrunk for lack of exercise. He was a blowhard without an instrument.

Like the prince who comes to the castle seeking to marry the princess but fails the king's three tests?

No, because there is, at least, a princess.

And because eventually one prince does succeed, although not without the assistance of magic.

For Raven to find his Honk, there is no magic.

Humans are up against a similar bit of pesky mythical chicanery: we keep striving to do the One Great Thing we know we must do but have never heard or seen an example of. And even if we had, we're not cut out to do this thing we try for, so we continue to hone our skills at accomplishing extremely difficult feats in place of it, some of them quite beside the point. An entire galaxy of activities pours out of us, but no Honk.

Raven reminds us that in some other universe there is Honk. We have all heard it in our genes, in the star-borrowed marrow of us. Raven will carry it in muffled form throughout the ages, like hunter-gatherers used to carry the embers of their fires wrapped in moss and hide when they moved camp from place to place. When the dark bird rows through the sky above us, softly displacing the air with his wing-flaps, yowping and creaking, those of us down below on the forest floor can nod a little and remember so many things we know: the color of the centaur's eye, sitting on the serpent's knee, . . .

Rewilding Religion

I am contented, for I know that Quiet
wanders laughing and eating her wild heart
among pigeons and bees.

— William Butler Yeats

There is a term ecologists use to describe one of their land-conservation strategies: rewilding.

For the lay person, the word means pretty much what it says: a plan for systematically re-introducing plant and animal species that would have been native to a land area at a much earlier time (before humans, ideally), but that have been crowded out by newer ones that humans brought along when they moved into the area.

As a poet, I want this word. "Rewilding" is a lovely, poetic idea, and I would like to commandeer it, with its riddlic fire, for immediate emergency application to contemporary Christianity, especially "the God question."

Poetry and religion share a common spiritual wellspring; it has always been in the interest of each for the other to thrive. But over time, some poets grew wary about expressing their religious passion in poems, lest they be misinterpreted as preaching a particular belief system. There is a porous but invisible net between the same words used in the differing rhetorics of persuasion: religious, political, or poetic. Some of these words, through centuries of proprietary use by religions, have been charged and saturated with certain specialized meanings. Now many poets are taking advantage of these essentially "pre-energized" words to add power and beauty to their work. This is not a new phenomenon; it's more like a return to a very ancient and beautiful relationship.

Over the past few years, a number of contemporary American poets have begun quite openly making rents in this invisible border by the use of religious vocabulary and spiritual insights in their work. This appears to happen in a spontaneous way, not because the poets are now "coming out of the closet" by daring to secularize an entire vocabulary that was previously regarded as sacred. It's much more honest, spontaneous, and subtle than that, having to do with a much enlarged understanding of terms like "holy" and "sacred," so that you can feel these concepts in the air even if the words themselves don't actually occur. I have gathered about twenty-one poets onto an informal list, and if I made a sustained, scholarly effort, I'm certain I could easily triple that number.

Once again, poetry is opening itself to potentially risky cross-pollination. This time it's "rewilding" itself with religion.

Christianity, on the other hand, seems insistent upon narrowing its definition of itself to the point that it risks drying up altogether.

I was brought up Catholic, and though I left the Church many years ago, I never lost my curiosity about religion, and by extension mythology, literature, anthropology, art history, archaeology, philosophy, and folklore, all disciplines that deal with how people envision themselves and their world.

Archaeologists, anthropologists, and other social scientists have known for quite some time that many "pagan" folk religions, with their accompanying stories and songs, never completely died out but simply went underground in a variety of ways. If you know how and where to look for evidence, you can find a huge variety of damaged fragments of the original animism that once covered most of the earth. This could be thought of as highly valuable patches of pristine cultural wilderness. We can use them as standards for our own spiritual "rewilding."

People are like plants: they keep their survival options open by employing a huge variety of basic strategies for getting through life as well as possible. Religion is simply one of these almost infinitely-variable strategies. Thus, I have been perpetually vexed by my own childhood religion's fixation on monotheism.

It took me about thirty years to decide, for

example, how to deal with the matter of category: believer, agnostic, or atheist? "None of the Above" has never been, and is not now, considered an option. Here's a story to help with that dilemma.

I've been arrested by the Thought Police in a fundamentalist dictatorship. Holding a knife to my throat, the thug-in-charge snarls, "Die, Atheist Pig!"

"But, sir [madam], I am not an atheist," I reply. Puzzled, the thug consults his phone: "You're lying! It says right here on the form you don't believe in God!"

"Yes, it's true I don't believe in God. But I'm not an atheist because that would mean I agree that the existence of God is the central defining religious question. And it most definitely is not. I don't even know what the word 'God' means, so I surely can't say anything about his (her) existence, and what's more, I'm not really interested."

At this point the thug in my story would roll his eyes, thrust his knife into his belt (the quality of his mercy not being strained) and toss me onto the wrong pile. The third one, for agnostics.

I might have shouted, "And I'm not an agnostic either!" but the story stops here. Monotheistically speaking, there are really only two piles to toss people into: the atheists and the believers.

Such a duality insults us all. To begin with, it shows a crass indifference to the first 100,000 years or so of human history when our ancestors lived in small groups, mostly outdoors, foraging and hunting in what we now call "the natural world." Monotheism doesn't seem to have occurred to them, nor apparently did the creation question govern their most urgent spiritual daily thoughts and activities. Yet they led lives that included a healthy variety of spiritual practices, rituals, and beliefs that resulted from the specific environments they spent centuries immersed in. In short, they had "wild" religion.

Every week I scan book reviews, essays, and other references hoping to find someone who will say, "Hey, this God question we've been asking — it's a red herring! Here are all the real questions we used to ask ourselves so very long ago." Instead, I keep finding nothing but the Two Sides. They line up something like this:

Side 1. If you are a Believer in one God (the option of polytheism is never mentioned) and follow some version of a hierarchical, faith-based religion, you're on the side that is both permitted and assumed to enjoy — in certain carefully rationed and scrutinized portions — faith, intuition, emotional depth, metaphor, dreams, divination, visions, mystery, and sudden blinding irrational insights that might lead to art.

Side 2. If you are an Atheist, your exclusive and proprietary stash includes all of science, mathematics, reason, clarity of thought, accuracy, numbers, empiricism, common sense, and the assumption that all talk of "spirits" or "spirituality" is superstition, a pesky holdover from earlier, more primitive times, from which science and technology have offered us, finally, welcome relief. Artistic abilities will be assumed to be a measurable product of brain chemistry.

There is nothing real in the argument; it leaves us trussed up inside a dessicated world where words are considered an acceptable substitute for experience. And experience, I would argue, is basically wordless. You don't need to argue about what you know because it's part of the part of you that you take with you everywhere you go. Like a wombat does, or a baobab tree.

If this sounds like a paradox, all it needs is a Side 3 to make the paradox dissolve.

As a poet, I would like to suggest an alternative approach to Side 1 and Side 2 mentioned above, and call it rewilding religion.

Poetry, as a kind of storehouse for the human imagination, has never lost its recessive capacity for all manner of essential foolishness. That is to say, poetry has always kept its wild heart intact. For poets, "rewilding" could be a name for the necessary daily discipline we must carry out to keep our work alive and fresh. Each poet has a specific version of this practice, this touching of the forehead to the ground from whence comes all life.

Among other aspects of their calling, poets have always carried forward a kind of original animism that in more recent centuries has grown branches like surrealism, fantasy, and magic. Now we seem to be in the process of adding contemporary Christianity to the mix. The poets are rewilding religion instead of the theologians, you might say.

Leaf Dancing

Here is what I see. An asphalt road winding uphill ahead of me, dappled by shadows from late summer trees. As I lean into a long right-hand curve, a large yellow leaf, probably a Bigleaf Maple, skitters out from the left side of the road directly into my path, like a pedestrian crossing without looking both ways for traffic.

Reaching the line in the middle of the road, it stops. It starts to spin—vertically, on its sturdy stem, so slowly at first, I don't recognize what is happening. But there is no mistaking that this leaf is fully upright and that it could not maintain this position at all if it were not twirling, even in the graceful, distracted way of a gamin princess.

Quickly I check the trees on either side, the tall grasses beside the road as well. They are motionless; there is no breeze. The leaf is dancing for some other reason. It wobbles a little, like a lopsided planet it begins to tip, but then with a rush of something like desperate ecstasy, it rights itself for that last three full seconds of fandango panache directly in front of the oncoming metal bumper that will soon destroy it.

I blink. I slow to a crawl while the leaf completes its last pirouette, falls over, and resumes a horizontal position on the pavement. Surely I have not just witnessed a blatant flouting of certain of the smaller laws of biology and physics! There may be no air moving in the vicinity, but I obviously failed to discern the maverick eddy prowling along the ground, small enough to lifted a single leaf and make it into a temporary puppet clown. Right?

But no, I've seen this happen before, and this time the boldness and clarity of the leaf's actions finally convinces me. That silly, fragile, skittish bit of flotsam out there has carried out an act of frivolity in pure form.

I don't know if leaves need to break away and dance from time to time, but they do it nonetheless. And could these sometime surreptitious botanical outbursts be simply another example of Nature's normal habit of redundancy, experimentation, excess? Or are the leaves actually getting away with something unauthorized? Either way is fine with me.

Grandfather Blue

A few evenings ago around dusk, I looked up and saw a great blue heron in silhouette.

Even when they're not technically "in silhouette," G. B. herons look that way since their qualifying blue — grayish and chimerical — hardly qualifies as a color at all. The bird itself is so ancient and regal that its name is probably placed into the modern "blue" spectrum as a courtesy; what we call its color is more like an immortalized patina reeking out from some vast realm between the feathers and bones where a whole lot of hanky-panky evolution took place that never got into the books.

The heron was chugging across the horizon toward his lonely night resting place. These incredibly noble birds are huge in comparison to, say, robins and blue jays and even crows or most hawks. But they don't command the jaw-dropping attention of golden eagles, magnificent frigate birds, or storks. Still, even though they're fairly common in most parts of the U.S., I will go to my death not ceasing to do a double take of awe and deep joy whenever I see one.

In this case, at this time, a word rolled down the marble-chute of my idle brain: grandfather. And I stuck out my lower lip as I squinted into the pale sky from which the sun had just withdrawn all its color flags and watched the almost ungainly progress of the bird into the place where I could no longer recognize its shape.

"What do you mean by grandfather?" I thought, and shook my head. "If this is a grandfather, he has no grandchildren. Nor is he going to sit and offer counsel to the younger members of his tribe. This person up there rowing along the runcinate line of low hills on my horizon — this guy is a grandfather all right, but not in the usual sense."

In what sense, then?

He . . . the heron could very well have been a "she" and thus would merit the term "grandmother," which word belongs in a story all its own, but I wasn't seeing it that way, and I can only tell this story . . . he was Grandfather partly because the bird had no idea that's what he was. His enormous innocence went along with him like an invisible cloak that had been made larger and larger and larger until it was very like a map of the world as big as the world. But his world. The great blue heron world. He is a bird and very firmly so. But not primarily.

Here my jaw did begin to drop. Yes, this heron

is "Grandfather," I can feel it in his particular silhouette, in his age, in his indifference, and most of all in what he knows we also know but don't know we know. He carries this knowledge with him everywhere. Perhaps this is why he flies so ponderously and slowly and with such archetypal authority that it makes you almost turn inside out when you see him.

But maybe we've been using the term "grandfather" flippantly all these years. Because the blue heron came first, with his own gradual accretion of survival behaviors and comic redundancies. He evolved from some reptilian ancestor and is probably closer to it than most (except for storks) birds. Does this in itself make him "Grandfather"? No, of course not. He started small and particular, but now he is working his way into being the head honcho of one of those huge word-bundles that ancient people used in their stories, and which we have tended to set aside. Certain sacred words act like codes, so that when you activate them, they send out signals along a variety of pathways, calling up the best meaning for the particular context at hand. Such words can be translated in a bewildering number of ways, but the context of each situation determines which translation the locals will recognize and imbibe at any particular moment. It's almost as if they had to sniff each meaning as it comes up to them before it is sanctioned for the particular situation.

Somehow, for me at least on this one evening,

the great blue heron earned the right to become, to represent, to embody an entire phalanx of meanings inside his specific avian self.

Like the ancient Greek word "Logos."

Or the word "Bayanay," which anthropologist Piers Vitebsky, in his book about the reindeer herding peoples of northeast Siberia, describes as:

> . . . a vast field of shared consciousness which encompassed the landscape as setting, as well as all the human and animal roles in the drama of stalking, killing, and consuming. This state of super-consciousness was so delicate and precarious that when talking of hunting, especially in the forest, one could not refer to animals by their ordinary names. Instead of the "crude" but "true" name kyaga, one referred to the bear as "abaga," meaning "grandfather." (Piers Vitebsky, *The Reindeer People: Living with Animals and Spirits in Siberia*, 2005, page 268.)

This, I understand, was something like the way I was receiving the spirit and personhood of that single heron crossing a strip of sky on a recent evening. Or, perhaps, that recent heron crossing a single sky on a strip of evening.

Scordatura: Upon Listening to Biber's *Rosary Sonatas*

Scordatura: Abnormal tuning of a stringed instrument in order to obtain unusual chords, facilitate difficult passages, or change the tone color.

—*Harvard Dictionary of Music*

Although I am a piano tuner who used to play a violin, I would not dream of referring to the violin as a simple instrument at the risk of calling down the ire of contemporary violin builders and their hefty spiritual ancestors, who might rant loudly to me in Italian in the middle of the night. Yet, from an instrument maker's point of view, a piano is much more difficult to build than a violin, a cello, even a harpsichord. But what means "simple"?

I have worked as a professional piano tuner for almost three decades. Because of the many tuning pins, and how deeply they are embedded into the pinblock, the job is lengthy, complicated, and physically demanding. For this reason, pianists have not tuned their own instruments since . . . well, possibly since the very beginning when the piano was conceived and presented to the world as a keyboard instrument totally different from a harpsichord. This presentation occurred in 1700 in Florence by the Medici family's chief musical instrument curator, Bartolomeo Cristofori.

But what means "complicated"?

Violins have only four strings that can be adjusted fairly quickly by the performers without the aid of tools. The pitches are easy to hear, and the traditional tuning places them a fifth apart. What could be simpler and more elegant? The music that comes out of these four strings is nonetheless phenomenal.

Most pianists have no idea that their pianos can be tuned in a variety of ways — hundreds, actually — because pianos have been tuned only one way for almost a hundred years. Similarly, many violinists have never heard of scordatura tuning, unless they play traditional fiddle music. As a preteen, I played classical and popular pieces on the violin, and my teachers never told me that GDAE was only one of many possible tuning patterns. I first learned of the renegade Italian tuning term at roughly the same age I became fully aware of the concept of sin.

Why would an instrument I considered to be almost holy ever be tuned abnormally on purpose? Why would anyone want to do that? My head would not wrap itself around the prospect, so I put it aside—as it turns out, for something like fifty years.

In the fifteen *Rosary Sonatas* by Heinrich Ignaz Franz Biber (1644–1704) for violin and unspecified accompanying instruments, the violin is tuned differently for each sonata, and fourteen of these tunings are scordatura.

This is a good word to roll around in your mouth, in your bad imitation of an Italian accent, and recognize as mildly wicked. Or, more to the point, to be reminded of something wicked. What? You can find the word in musical dictionaries alongside more familiar terms such as adagio, allegro, piano, and there you discover why the "scord" part gives you a little shiver: it began life as the Italian word *discordare*, which even today still means "out of tune." In English we say "discord," meaning anything from a family argument to "an inharmonious combination of musical tones sounded together." But somewhere in the early seventeenth century, the Italian word *discordare* labored and brought forth— perhaps we should say discarded—a fledgling that flourished for roughly a hundred years as a name for a particular kind of beauty, rather than just a general term for its opposite.

Furthermore, in the seventeenth century, when this deliberate abnormal—meaning atypical, but not bad or ugly—tuning of non-keyboard stringed instruments (lutes, guitars, viols, and the members of the violin family) was in common use among composers and performers, the normal, or "*accordare*" way of tuning was not so widely agreed upon and rigidly followed as it is today. In fact, some stringed instruments (viola d'amore, for example) had no single "*accordare*" tuning standard to deviate from. Not only was the music improvised on these small instruments, but so was the very scale structure upon which the music found its rest. This means that for a hundred years or so, a large body of stringed instruments in Europe were regularly permitted, cajoled, and urged over an extra threshold in order to make their music. It was that kind of threshold that angels are especially loathe to cross.

Keyboard instruments, in order to make music, also must be tuned by some physically dictated guidelines. But harpsichords, clavichords, and pianos have many more strings than violins, lutes, viols, or guitars. As a result, a tuning pattern— also called a temperament—for keyboards is quite a difficult thing to settle upon. There is no orthodoxy here; any temperament will be based on a somewhat whimsical core idea rather than one firmly sanctioned by the physical harmonies of musical acoustics. Thus, all keyboard tunings are, in a sense, scordatura. But this, of course, is a total paradox. How can you diverge from "normal" if there is nothing normal to diverge from?

Scordatura has now revealed an odd symmetry. A violinist has the option of tuning her instrument either the normal way, or not. The orthodox tuning has the pattern GDAE, which is based on the natural harmonics of musical strings, and has been sanctioned over and over again by the demanding ears of musicians throughout many centuries. Hence, any deliberate deviations from this pattern would require moving away from an easy and traditional purity. On keyboard instruments— organs, harpsichords, clavichords, pianos— such easy purity is not physically possible. Nonetheless, a series of twelve perfect fifths remains the mathematical and musical template that all keyboard temperaments aspire to, in theory.

So, the odd symmetry goes like this: the violins don't stick with perfection even though they know they can have it any time; the keyboards keep trying to counterfeit such perfection even though they know they can't ever have it. The "abnormal" tuning of a violin in scordatura and the "abnormal" tuning of a keyboard in one of many possible temperaments represent two distinct aesthetic impulses. Like two different reasons for misbehaving. Not only that, but two different beautiful reasons.

When Biber composed the *Rosary Sonatas* in honor of the sufferings and ecstasies of the Blessed Virgin Mary, he specified fourteen scordatura tunings and one usual one. A scordatura tuning involves tightening or loosening one or more of the strings to change the pitch from the normal pattern, in increments of a half or whole tone. This can be done to expand the range of the instrument or to make certain passages easier (or even possible) when the performer is playing double stops, for example.

In this composition, Biber was using scordatura also, or perhaps only, for a third reason: by deliberately and radically pushing the physical limits of the instrument so that it would seem to be speaking from a variety of highly emotion-charged responses, he would bring about a mystical union between the performer, the listener, and the larger, holy story being thus musically sanctified.

Tightening strings makes the violin sound harder, closer to what we would call nasal or keening; loosening strings brings about a weaker, more husky or throaty sound. By varying these effects, Biber jerks the listener around through a turmoil of conflicting aesthetic responses based merely on the tuning, never mind what the music itself is doing. This adds an entire dimension to music that we have lost, a dimension that can set a first-time listener almost staggering.

For example, in the "Ascension," Biber set out the pattern CEGC, which means the bottom G is raised three whole tones and the top E is lowered two. These alterations mess with the violin's physics in intriguing and disturbing and marvelous ways that go beyond beautiful or ugly. Biber is drawing the instrument, by a variety of paths, close to the brink of noise. The notes themselves are normal enough, but each alternation of string tension changes the violin's voice. You hear the instrument speaking regular words in an irregular tone of voice, like a mother right on the edge of a breakdown. You begin to receive a very ancient message directly through your sinews as they engage harmonically with those of the stressed-out instrument. Your sense of music, and of suffering, is enlarged.

Because only two instruments are playing—violin and accompanying keyboard—and because both are mistuned according to their symmetrically opposite physical responses to the rules of musical physics, something pristine can take place. The listener is forced to hear that the violin by nature operates in a different space than the harpsichord does; they render different realities. As if the fact that they are musical instruments is not precisely the essential element of their ensuing actions. As if, unknown to us, music was actually born twice. Our attention is drawn to music as a raw material rather than as an art, and even though we can continue to rest on the assumption that this familiar and beloved phenomenon we have always taken for granted has to do with sound, we begin to acknowledge that more than one member of the Grendel family of music is out there stalking the world, and we have hitherto never run into its mother. Apparently, at least two different gods had the music idea at the same time and released it through two different doors: the up and the down doors, perhaps? The division door and the multiplication door. Magnitude and multitude? Like Homer's two gates for dreams.

One recent night I dreamed that my son Timothy (now in his mid-forties), at age two, wandered away from the glassed-in spaceship we were occupying, out into the alien, tropical landscape of an earth-like planet. I was half asleep on a divan (not a sofa), and when he went out I lulled myself into complacency by noticing that he was accompanied by a young man employed inside our vehicle. Gradually, reason nudged me into full wakefulness by reminding me that this employee was not hired to be a babysitter and certainly was not responsible for my child. By this time it was dusk, and there was no sign of my little son or the young man. I cried "Tim!" in increasing panic, and eventually he showed up whitely in the dim light.

I woke up stifling from guilt and nostalgia. The dream had called up a similar scene from years ago. I was looking out the window into the backyard where Tim and his older brother were just coming up through the trees toward the house. Patrick, my older son, was not yet visible, but for some reason Tim glowed just a little as he rustled over the grass in his paper diapers; his little fat knees caught at my heart like candles. I was overwhelmed with love and with the simple beauty of the scene. But also, I remember, by that irrational dark that afflicts all mothers, the fear of losing the child. More than that, I felt, as I did in the dream, guilt for not paying enough attention to the possibilities of children wandering off. But how silly! My sons are alive despite all the mistakes, the accidents, the near-misses that actually took place during the time their father and I were bringing them up. I never seriously neglected my children. Why should a simple dream, a simple glance out the window remind me of things that never actually happened. At some base level of human existence, all possible actions and outcomes do become equally likely, no longer beautiful or ugly, good or bad, but deeply, whimsically, terrifyingly available. The dream reminded me of that, as did the *Rosary Sonatas* when I listened to them for the first time, also on a recent night.

How powerful is a rendition of scordatura tunings when presented in such a piece of music! The simple result in this case is two different versions of beauty trading places in the listener's ear throughout the performance, like figure and ground. But here, in the violin part, the voice of the instrument is being permitted to insert a primal response to the fundamental circumstances in which it is designed to make music: like a dialect of wood and gut. Even by late seventeenth-century performance standards, where highly difficult performance tricks were routinely inserted by composers and performers as if they were competing athletes, Biber's scordatura tunings are considered extraordinary in the level of "suffering" they imposed upon performer and instrument alike. Yet the only extant hand-written version of these "Mystery Sonatas" is apparently not the original; there seem to be no contemporary published copies. The first known published version (1905) is said to be full of errors, and how would anybody know?

Perhaps this is as it should be. If there is no final, no authorized version, the piece forever offers the excitement of ultimate possibility: of at least two opportunities for exquisite secrecy, for nuanced pain, for reasons for things. This happens so casually by the mere tightening or loosening of four strings. Or rather, so gratuitously. Through our ears, which are a direct pathway to the self, we are helpless and even terrified before such a simple manifestation of infinity.

But then, with so much infinity expressly, if fleetingly, available, might this not suggest more than one essential way through the world? Perhaps if beauty arises out of the Is-ness of things, spontaneously, irrevocably, and if this Is-ness exists hugely, obliviously but all around at all times, we need only a tiny shift in the magnification of our seeing or hearing, a minuscule twitch of angle, and it will explode into us: a series of caverns inside the veins of each leaf, the lavish turquoise bleedings from the under-surface of the sea. If this is so, then how can suffering be merely what it seems?

Instructions for Walking Through Walls

In walking through walls, you cannot go swiftly forward. Although the substance you are up against is in the act of changing its core identity from being "a wall" to being "a so-called wall," nonetheless it will not ultimately attain any more fluidity or transparency than that of a very thick dust. And this dust will not conveniently morph into fire or rain as it gives way before you. Thus a wholly different set of skills and body parts is needed from the ones you commonly employ in simply . . . walking.

And, in fact, to temporarily lapse into the technicalities of this operation, you must move forward by virtue of a gradual tilt away from active and toward passive behavior. Something begins to occur in conjunction with, but not directly caused by, your focused intention. We might call it a constant realigning of proportional valences. This will present itself, eventually, as the re-emergence of one of many probable phylogenies that have lingered, dormant and redundant, somewhere in your body all your life. It's a natural part of your shadow-self, an inflatable emergency raft under your seat that can be activated if you carefully read paragraph 3-b on page 17 of the instructions conveniently squashed into the bottom of the seat pocket in front of you.

In other words, humans have always been capable of walking through walls, and sometimes they find themselves, out of rare necessity, remembering how to do it.

(Hint: You can practice ahead of time; for example, by repeatedly pressing the bent second joint of your pinky finger very gently against the front side of a closed piano keyboard.)

I had no time to practice. In late January, my chronically homeless forty-six-year-old son needed emergency dental work, and the only way he could get it was to come and stay with me in my tiny duplex for five weeks. The two of us had not spent more than four or five hours in one another's company for the last twenty years, and our occasional telephone conversations had been an ordeal for both of us. The only way we were each going to survive this searing initiation into a new relationship was for each of us to spend a lot of time walking through walls.

Morning. I wake up at my usual 5:30 and politely

lie in bed for an hour before I pass quietly through the living room where he is lying asleep on the sofa, and begin to grind coffee in the kitchen (no door to block out the noise). He gets up off the sofa without a word, goes into my study, shuts the door, and lies down on the floor to grab an extra few hours of sleep. He usually stays up until two or three in the morning, high on caffeine and energy drinks, while I normally go to bed shortly after nine.

Thus begins our daily dance. It's January in western Oregon, which means it's raining outside. Aside from trips to the grocery store and a few damp hikes in the rain forest, we are stuck inside a 690-square-foot house together, day after day, waiting for the medicaid-funded clinics to grind through the process at their own pace. When I come into a room, he goes into another one. When I sit down to dinner, he waits till I'm done. He goes through a loaf of bread and a half pound of butter per day. He makes endless cups of coffee and tea, which he leaves on flat surfaces all over the house. He listens to my phone conversations and gets angry if I talk to his father. We switch places at my computer desk, hour by hour. I cook endless meals; he helps with the dishes if I ask him, but never thinks of it on his own.

But he also pulls an enormous stack of books off my shelves and piles them on the end of the coffee table by my rocking chair, where he sits reading and taking notes. Sometimes he asks me a question and we have a spurt of conversation that lasts half an hour. I almost never mention an author or a book that he doesn't know something about. He has gotten much of his recent education from browsing Little Free Libraries all over the city of Portland, which he has walked from one end to the other, day and night, carrying his sleeping bag, backpack, and a smaller bag for his camera gear.

A week after he arrives, when he has had a root canal and temporary crown, we drive together to the center of our city to take part in the local version of the Women's March. I had no idea in advance what his politics would be. But he says he voted for Hillary Clinton (I had mailed his ballot to his usual general delivery address). It's obvious there will be no parking anywhere near the beginning of the march, so we walk about two miles before we even begin "marching." Neither of us has a sign. We blend in easily with the crowd filling the street in both directions as far as I can see.

"Wow!" I tell him, "This is way bigger than all the other marches we've had here. Must be at least a thousand people." The newspaper account the next day said there were seven thousand. The largest demonstration our city has ever experienced.

Then, when we were standing in the rain chanting and singing with the other people, including many children, all of them peaceful and smiling, polite yet determined, I suddenly remembered the Vietnam War march in Washington, D.C. in November, 1969. Again, the streets were filled with people on all sides, as far as we could see. It was bitter cold, but we were hugely motivated.

I turned to my firstborn son with a grin. "Do you know, this is the second demonstration we have marched in together," I told him. "You came along with me during the last one because I was pregnant with you!"

He thought that was cool. We walked through another wall together.

Song of Songs: A Contemporary Poet Takes a Look at an Old Poem

My husband has translated the Song of Songs from the ancient Hebrew. It's not as if this hasn't been done before. Why has he carried through with this difficult task? He's not sure exactly, but feels driven by an emotional attachment to the work. This could mean that his decades of immersion in the Hebrew Bible have laid down a set of instincts upon the contours of his inner geography, and these instincts, which are likely rare and formidable in their specialized capabilities, are telling him something is still lacking, something is still there to be found.

I respect that. He asked me to help him because I am a poet. I am also an editor for a small poetry publishing collective, a long-time amateur translator, and essayist.

But perhaps more importantly, I come cold into this work. I do not carry with me the usual Christian baggage of prior familiarity and reverence for the Hebrew Bible. I grew up Catholic and never read the "Old Testament" because Catholicism tends to emphasize the New. I never read the Song of Songs before this year, and I approach it with the critical eye of a poetry lover, hungry for beauty anywhere it is said to show up.

I remain an outsider in this enterprise. Yet reading various translations of this ancient set of love poems, as well as conversing with my husband about his work in progress, has overflowed into a set of questions and observations that may contribute something useful to the ongoing scholarship.

Preliminary Assumption: Poetry is Formal Speech

One of my personal core assumptions about poetry is that it's innately formal. Not all contemporary poets would say that, but oddly enough, the general public would agree with me. The large segment of the public that does not habitually read or listen to poetry still believes wistfully in the existence of a separate, poetic speech, just as I do. The difference is that most people regard "it rhymes" as the only required formality to turn ordinary speech into a poem. And for the result to be a good poem, it must not contain "fancy words" — i.e., too many adjectives or terms you have to look up in the dictionary.

In approaching the Song of Songs as an ancient collection of love poems, therefore, I assume that its composer(s) and listeners were engaged in an age-old conspiracy to enter a special rhetorical space — a poetry space — whenever any part of this work was being performed. And bearing down with that assumption a bit more heavily, I assume that the Song of Songs shares with all (or most) ancient oral-tradition poetry the convention that inside this rhetorical space prevails an entire secondary vocabulary apparatus special to the occasion. This is a distinct and stable convention, practiced and honed over thousands of years. What it condones is that "metaphor" is primary in poetic speech. That is, poetic code words do not substitute a second meaning for what we would say in "ordinary everyday" or "common" speech, but rather the poetic code is understood to mean what it says on its own terms. As if everybody knows everything in the world by two distinct, but totally equal languages, and can switch them at will. As if Adam's naming of the creatures in the garden was a bit of a sly joke because someone else — maybe Eve? — was later authorized to name them again.

Love poetry is especially well suited to flourish

within such a rhetorical space; since the entire society is part of the conspiracy, all you have to do is call up the poetry trolley, and automatically you all enter the safe house of the other words where you're not violating the kinds of rules that might exist outside that space, that sanctuary.

In this sense, the obvious use of "code words" in the Song of Songs signifies a switch from everyday mode to poetic mode of speech, and it happens en masse as soon as the poem is brought into whatever public listening space wherein it was usually celebrated.

Second Assumption: This is a Set of Poems from the Oral Tradition

I'm assuming that these poems formed themselves inside their culture by the usual crucible of human needs, whims, passions, and influences from surrounding cultures. I assume they were well-worn by centuries of speaking before this particular group was "called in," so to speak, and written down. Very little scholarly work has been done about lyric oral poetry; the great body of oral tradition scholarship builds upon Lord and Parry's work, which dealt with narrative epic, and though there is some related scholarship regarding shorter works such as ballads (Roderick Beaton); grieving ceremony narratives (Steven Feld); poems and stories still active in the oral mode as nascent fragments of longer, more epic-like tales (Harold Scheub); I don't know of work that focuses on oral-tradition lyric poetry, and most especially love poems.

For my purposes in bringing a critical eye to the Song of Songs, I must assume it to be a somewhat random collection of individual pieces, preserved by a huge stroke of luck. The poems strongly suggest to me the kind of repetition that would come from many different versions of the same little scene or situation. In other words, this collection swims into view as if it were a musical composition called a theme and variations. The poems work as a group depository of readily interchangeable ardent, exuberant, young adult love statements. To view the work this way frees me from certain expectations I would have if I thought a single poet were responsible. I can stop asking myself: "Is this high quality poetry by the standards of its time, never mind the standards of today?" And instead, I can listen to the poem in a variety of ways, always remembering we might not even understand the nature of the excellence of this work, always remembering that "theme and variations" can be a generative strategy, and for sure there is a feeling that something new and vital may have been struggling to crawl out from the "rhetorical space" in which these poems seem to have been festering.

Final Assumption: This is Real Poetry

If poetry is to differ from prose, there has to be a reason. Much contemporary English-language poetry is really prose that uses line breaks to disguise it as poetry. Many poets are unable to summon the instincts that would allow them to reactivate ancient speech-generated proportional, tradition-sanctioned rhythms that signify the switch from an "ordinary" to "poetic" mode of speech. Poetic language is in the muscles and bones; it can't be imposed by a set of rules. We are a nation of people with ill-educated poetic bones, both for reading and composing poetry.

So how can we make an informed literary judgment about this ancient poem, especially when it's translated into English? In Hebrew, I am told by my husband and by other translators, the poem bristles with sound play, parallelisms, alliteration, enjambment, assonance, and other such prosodic devices, so there is no doubt that these are at least poems.

Informed instinct must be the final arbiter as to the quality of a work of art. I can only say, finally, that I do not know why this set of poems "gets through" to me, despite the many limits that the tradition seems to have imposed, particularly the repetitions of generalities such as beautiful, delicious, sweet; and also the somewhat wooden repetitions of code words such as deer, gazelles, goats, a variety of herbs, flowers and fruits, as well as a list of royal-treasury valuables such as ivory and silver.

Because of these vocabulary limitations, the poems can seem adolescent, naive, as if they were the product of a rural and illiterate peasant class who may, like the folks Theocritus heard in third-century-B.C. Sicily, have amused themselves by engaging in singing matches in which they mixed actual experience with romanticized notions of far-off worlds they had only heard about in stories

As with the so-called "formulas" of Homeric and other oral-epic poetry, what might seem to be the greatest weakness is actually the greatest strength. I'm making that assumption about codes and parallelisms in the Song of Songs.

Parallelism, as it shows up in English translations of ancient poetry, tends to bore modern readers because we see it as a sign of awkward redundancy. Translators often suppress or even outright ignore this device when they are trying to turn the old poetry into something exciting by contemporary terms. Parallelisms are sprinkled through the Song of Songs: sometimes within a single line ("my love, my friend," "like a gazelle, my lover, a young deer," "My dove, in the rock's clefts / in secret, in the cliff"); or in a two-line stanza ("a bundle of myrrh, my lover / a henna cluster, my lover," "on his wedding day / the day of his heart's joy," "I was asleep / but my heart stayed awake"); or it can take up an entire quatrain: ("I sought my life's love / sought, but didn't find him / —I scarcely passed them / when I found my love."). Examples abound.

Here's why I think parallelism is more than a "mere device," to quote James Thurber from *The Thirteen Clocks*. Because of the nature of language, no two words ever mean exactly the same thing. Therefore, laying down a synonym within a formal structure like poetry causes a kind of nuclear fission, wherein an entire universe of possibility is laid open to the mind of the listener. Instead of clumsily reinforcing a single denotation, a parallelism hints at an infinity of directions out and thus allows a simple truism to hold onto the full power of its original meaning, because the words, when reinforced by their close relatives, will not wear out. Thus you can get away with saying "I love you," and it will still pack some punch.

The same principle, I believe, holds true in the other chief poetic device that comes across in translation, which is the use "codes" in the Song of Songs. Because these are love poems, and because they are highly unusual in that the male and female lovers speak to one another directly and as equals, it might be expected that a code language would be needed to prevent the "grown-ups" on the outside from discovering what was really going on.

This seems unlikely for a number of reasons, but mostly because the code words do not function like equations, like similes, where it is relatively simple to nudge and wink and say, "Oh, yes, 'graze among the lilies' obviously means oral sex," and so forth. The possibilities for such one-on-one connections abound: nard, ivory, grapes, garden, vineyard, pomegranate, gazelle.

After puzzling over these code words for quite some time, I have come to respect them as a sign of high poetic skill, of a kind we no longer use in quite the same way. For the most part, the codes seem not to operate as similes or metaphors in quite the way we use them today. Rather, they act as "switching devices" to keep listeners constantly and vibrantly aware that they are inside an enclosed rhetorical space. Within this space, the code words fall to and flex themselves almost like small physical beings, almost like the language used in Old English riddles, where the solution to the riddle remains baffling because it never was meant to be obvious. Even for the original composers and listeners, there was always a gap, an ambiguity in the equation between the tenor and the vehicle, between the code word / phrase and its referent. This is actually the core of the creative vitality that remains evident in the Song of Songs. Language is felt to be crawling out from under words, as it always does.

Thus, even though the Song of Songs can seem, to a modern lover of poetry, to be tiresomely naive in its use of sanctioned formalities and tiresomely lacking in the daring poetic leaps from inner to outer realities that we relish today, nonetheless it qualifies as fine poetry because its limited language has carved out its own mode of operation within the rhetorical space allotted to it. Because the Song of Songs developed within an "assumption of poetry," it found a way to behave as poetry. And, of course, as always happens when poetry is given an inch, it immediately takes a mile.

Hummingbirds in the Garden

I didn't plan it this way, but it turns out that my backyard garden has the exact number of flowers in it to support one hummingbird. No more. No less.

The configuration goes roughly thus: moving from shade to sun, two bleeding heart bushes surrounded by salvia, give way to a large clump of bee balm, followed almost immediately by a thick stand of flaming red crocosmia. Here the vegetable section begins, and most years I accomplish the segue with a trellis of scarlet runner beans.

This entire segment of red-flowers-with-long-seductive-throats is about twenty feet, surrounded and interrupted by yellow dahlias, white peonies, daphne, purple pincushion flower, yarrow, pink hollyhocks, and some gorgeous clumps of stuff I can no longer remember the names of.

The original plan was to have a garden biased in favor of hummingbirds — plural.

The two hummingbird species that show up here in western Oregon's Willamette Valley every summer, Anna's and Rufous, each measure barely four inches from head to tail and are about half as wide through the tummy. They expend a tremendous amount of energy beating their wings at seventy times per second so they can hover like tiny helicopters in front of every single flower, sometimes flying backwards or vertically in order to poke their beaks straight up into a downward-drooping blossom.

During the high summer season when the little hummers get most of their nutrition from nectar, they're on a constant sugar high, which gives them a ferocious amount of energy to get rid of. Nonetheless (so common lore has it), they live on a knife-edge balance between the amount of energy their bodies can store compared to the amount they must expend in the normal (insanely) active process of feeding themselves. So yes, hummingbirds are focused; they do not pootle.

Nonetheless, they do engage in extra-curricular activities, and this I find very puzzling.

If Nature were the well-honed Darwinian machine we are led to believe it is, these hummingbirds would be constrained to behave like wind-up toys, moving deftly and with the least amount of excess motion from flower to flower. Their little brains would be clicking like abacuses as they progressed through their territory, constantly re-calculating the shortest distance between two points so they wouldn't get all fagged out by making a long detour around the apple tree on the way to the sweet peas — for example.

Instead, these silly poppets fritter half their energy away every day by chasing each other around the garden in huge loopy circles while chittering at the top of their lungs. Their favorite game might well be called Hummingbird-in-the-Manger, by which I mean if one hummingbird is quietly sipping and a second one inserts even the tip of her beak over the hedge from the next yard, the first one is off like a flash to chase her out.

I truly cannot see how this never-finish-a-meal-in-peace behavior serves any real survival purpose. They don't seriously fight. They are simply driven to stand their ground — pardon the expression — above all else. Yet the primary impression given by the pugnacious little ritual is that both birds are having a high old time.

Of course, these eejits (as the British like to say) who behave as if they were working out in a CrossFit gym obviously thrive despite this daily energy-squandering routine. I do not come across exhausted bodies scattered about on the grass like electric cars that didn't make it to the next charging station on time.

In summer, at any rate, the energy of these tiny birds must be something close to nuclear in its fission capacities. One atom of bee-balm nectar equals ten seconds flying at twenty m.p.h. almost straight up and then zipping diagonally across the whole garden, only to come to a halt on a holly twig in the next yard, scarcely winded and ready for the next round.

I suppose the "purpose" of these seemingly suicidal digressions from the serious business of staying alive would be keeping the little birds fit, either for their long migration—as in the case of Rufous—or, as with the Anna's who stay here all winter, to withstand the long cold months stuck with a diet of bugs and lichen.

But I really don't think so. I think Nature has an infinity of stops, pulls them all out, and some creatures choose "all of the above" and damn the consequences.

Last week I went out and bought a juicer. I want to learn to fly straight up.

April Fools' Day 1996 at the Amtrak Station in Atlanta, Georgia

I am lightheaded with fever. This means when things start going wrong, I don't even notice. I lug my overstuffed suitcase-without-wheels through all the temporary construction tunnels at the Atlanta airport to get down to ground level; I go outside into the frigid April breeze and stand for half an hour with all the other puzzled and shivering people in the carousel of shuttle vans, and I don't feel even a blip of irritation. Why didn't they tell me I would need a sweater in Atlanta? Why are there too many people to fit into each van? And why am I always at the end of the line? The Olympics don't even start for another three months.

The driver snickers when I tell him I'm going to

the Amtrak station. He doesn't bother to ask what time my train leaves. The other people are all going to hotels like the Hilton and the Sheraton, which is what you're supposed to be doing in an airport van, so we drive them to their hotels first, all eight of them, one at a time. This takes about an hour and a half, during which we tour most of Atlanta. "You think things are bad now?" says the driver sardonically (he has a sardonic mustache). "Already we're getting traffic for the Olympics. Already!"

"What if my train were leaving in fifteen minutes?" I mutter to myself. But who would go to a train station from an airport? The Atlanta airport probably occupies five thousand acres and employs a bajillion taxi and van drivers and caterers and shopkeepers and airline mechanics and ticket agents and security personnel. The Amtrak station dozes shabbily in a hollow on a downtown corner, with parking for about a dozen cars. It is possible to reach it by bus from the airport, but first you have to take the subway, then get off at the Art Center and transfer to Bus #23 while lugging your (my) ancient suitcase. The subway system is attached to the airport basement like a sucker fish onto its host, pulling people down from the sky to continue their travels beneath the earth. But not to the train station.

I am deposited at the Amtrak station two hours early for my train. "How can this be?" you might well ask. Because there are only two trains per day, the southbound in the morning and the northbound in late afternoon. The airplane schedules exist in a different world than that of trains. I'm beginning to think my romantic notion of chugging directly into the station at Clemson, South Carolina, scarcely two miles from my parents' house — my mother and father waiting on the platform — may have become like an old home movie that ends with a great flashing of black and white dots, and then oblivion. But then, I do have a mild fever.

When I walk into the train station, I notice two waiting rooms, one smaller than the other. I suppose this is leftover from the days of segregation. A black woman with her active little boy are the only other people in the station. They are sitting in the small room, so I feel inclined to sit there too, at least for awhile. The benches "out there" are larger, like old church pews, with high backs and ample seats. The benches "in here" have those stupid little dividers, so you can't stretch out your feet.

Despite my fever, I decide I'm up for this. I pull out my notebook to work on a poem. I set my lumpy baggage in front of me like a hassock, remove my Birkenstock sandals to put on some socks against the chill, take a slug of water from my water bottle, and feel quite competent. I look up at the cobwebs on the enormous round window at the end of the room and at the thin April light coming in through its opaque white panes. If I keep my chin up I might almost believe I'm in a cathedral. But when my chin comes down, I see the old-timey vending machines, and I simply must go and get myself a cup of that vile coffee with the powdered milk that comes out scalding hot into a Styrofoam cup. I buy some peanut butter crackers, the ones of a color between orange and yellow, a color food should not be.

An hour goes by and more people come in. My head starts to ache. A pleasant young ticket office employee is circulating among the waiting crowd, letting each of us know personally that the train is an hour late. This is not a dream. I start to walk around the outer room. I keep excusing myself as I step over the extended legs of an old couple. Finally I stop to talk to them. They tell me they are going to New York. Their luggage is discreetly scruffy; they seem accustomed to long waits.

I look out through the back door along the platform to the tracks far below the station, the empty tracks. I am in a glass cage. A man in a red shirt goes out this door. Soon I see him making wide gestures with his cigarette. He is standing on the edge of an abyss. The woman doing crossword puzzles has not looked up for an hour now. A taxi driver comes in, asking for a wheel chair. "There's a big woman out there, a really big one!" he says. They wheel her in, and she heaves herself onto the wide bench, leans back, covers her face with a cowl.

Children are going through contortions on the benches. Two young men talk in Spanish across an aisle. A man and woman speak German over by the water fountain. The young ticket agent makes regular appearances. He talks briefly with the fat lady, coaxing her out from under her scarf, talks to the crossword-puzzle lady, to a restless and sweaty young man seated by the cigarette machine. "It's coming, it's coming!" he assures us all with a big grin, and we think to ourselves, "April Fool!"

Some old music is trapped above the ceiling fan, where it gabbles and hisses to itself like a bumblebee unable to escape through a window. I try to listen to it, but its edges have run amok, as if long ago someone forgot to turn it off. One day maybe it will wear itself completely out and dry up into a fine dust that will rain down from the ceiling and make the passengers sneeze. Gone will be another tradition from the Day of the Train.

The train is now an hour and a half late. This is not a dream. I stand at the front window looking out into the city. Across the street is a pancake house. Should I go out for a walk? In Athens, Greece, I probably would. Maybe even in Madrid, or Tokyo. But this is the Amtrak station in Atlanta, Georgia. I have a fever. This feels more like a prison than a cathedral.

Through the thick city dusk in front of the station, a man jogs slowly down the sidewalk. He turns his head our way, looks at me for a second or two through the window. He will carry my eyes as seeds in himself to disburse through the world, as I will carry his. That thought occupies me for quite some time. Everybody has looked at someone who has looked at someone, clear back to Adam and Eve. Thus are we all connected.

The station employees want to go home. "Let's party!" says one of the young Spanish-speaking men. He is sort of talking about all of us, sort of not. "Is this April Fools' Day, or what?" says the father of one of the energetic children. People are taking it all philosophically instead of getting angry. There's a general tendency for conversation. People are looking at one another more often, making exaggerated grimaces and shrugs. This is where the Olympics will take place in a few months. It's an election year. The time is out of joint. I am lightheaded with fever. If we stay here much longer, we'll probably all be in love.

Life in the Country

I go to bed thinking about Jorge Luis Borges,
who may have once heard a bird singing by
night on the outskirts of Barracas, and felt
compassion just exactly in the size of that bird.
— Václav Cílek, *To Breathe with Birds*

On a rainy afternoon in April, while house-sitting
for a friend in the middle of a woods twenty miles
south of Eugene, Oregon, I was eating a late
light lunch of fresh snapper, chard, and turnips —
snapper quick-fried in lemon, salt, and olive
oil; turnips and chard steamed together then
sprinkled with balsamic honey vinegar. No music
was playing from the radio; no electronic screen
devices were turned on. I was alone in a silent
room, a condition we might call "a natural state."

Toward the middle of the meal, a portion of
the chopped turnips began to migrate to the rim
of my plate, and though I had not consciously

made a decision about their fate, I had a sudden presentiment that they were doomed to remain uneaten through no fault of their own.

I mention this only because it surprised me that the weak premonitory vision did not immediately snuff itself out as such images generally do, but rather hung around as if it were an emissary from a distant country seeking an audience with the local sovereign. Pay attention! it was saying to me, and what the heck? How often does a person have both the time and the inclination to offer an audience to such an undeveloped notion as this?

I wrinkled my brow as if I were a person who had mislaid her capacity for language and turned my head very slightly to regard the edge of my plate with its stalwart little collection of rapidly-cooling veggies, soon to be tipped into the compost bin beside the sink. I felt neither guilt nor pity; rather it seemed as if I were part of a painting as it was being painted. I could feel our little tableau observed, and, briefly, to be sure, but quite firmly, recorded. Fish, chard, turnips, plate, person, large windows, pine forest, blotches of pale sky, April lurking and whisking her sibilant cloak.

Everything equal inside the painter's mind, no praise or blame.

This is what can happen when you move into an empty house in the middle of a pine woods in early spring three miles from the nearest small town (pop. 501) and its attendant interstate highway, although you can hear the traffic like a low sighing of wind in the trees whenever you walk out the front door. Despite the shooting range "down the road" that keeps alive the reminder that we are not currently in a war zone but that an entire population of humans dearly wishes we were and does its best to compensate for the loss. Although these noises bother me at a certain level, most of the usual din of civilization is absent out here, and this allows me to remember that there is a core silence in the ground and that I can feel it with my feet more clearly than with my ears.

Hence, my hierarchy of daily actions is being gradually skewed into a new shape. An old shape, I probably should say, but way before my recent memory. Either you're a person who can stand silence, or you're not. I wasn't sure which one I was anymore, but the fish-chard-turnip episode pretty much let me know that I'm a silence junkie after all. I can feel the base of my brain flaring out gently like one of the white trillium blossoms now appearing all over the forest floor. I feel like Alice in Wonderland outgrowing her house, her head poking up through the chimney. New possibilities are sprouting inside my heart as if it were a forest floor itself, once more chastened and receptive to the green fuzz that has quite simply overcome the twigs, brown pine needles, and leaves of the previous season; they have not left, they have been overlain. This goes on all the time. Blossoms are, in the end, cumulative, just as our memories are, our ecstasies, our flashes of love. That they seem to disappear is an illusion. They have moved to another spot on the plate.

About the Author

 Born under the sign of Libra, Anita Sullivan cheerfully admits to a life governed by issues of balance and harmony. This likely led to her career as a piano tuner, as well as her love of birds (Libra is an air sign), gardening, music, and fine literature. She spent years trying to decide if she was a piano tuner who wrote poetry or a poet who tuned pianos. She traveled a lot without becoming a nomad; taught without becoming a teacher; danced without becoming a dancer; fell totally in love with the high desert country of the Southwest and promptly moved to the Pacific Northwest rainforest. She has previously published two essay collections, a novel, two poetry chapbooks, and a full-length poetry collection. She was a founding member of the Portland, Oregon, poetry publishing collective Airlie Press.

• www.anitasullivan.org